30 Chic Days at Home

Self-care tips for when you have to stay at home, or any other time when life is challenging

FIONA FERRIS

Copyright © 2020 Fiona Ferris
www.howtobechic.com
All rights reserved.

ISBN: 9798663035248

Other books by Fiona Ferris

Thirty Chic Days: *Practical inspiration for a beautiful life*

Thirty More Chic Days: *Creating an inspired mindset for a magical life*

Thirty Slim Days: *Create your slender and healthy life in a fun and enjoyable way*

Financially Chic: *Live a luxurious life on a budget, learn to love managing money, and grow your wealth*

How to be Chic in the Winter: *Living slim, happy and stylish during the cold season*

A Chic and Simple Christmas: *Celebrate the holiday season with ease and grace*

The Original 30 Chic Days Blog Series: *Be inspired by the online series that started it all*

The Chic Author: *Create your dream career and lifestyle, writing and self-publishing non-fiction books*

Treinta Días Chic: *Inspiración practica para una vida hermosa (Spanish Edition)*

FIONA FERRIS

Contents

Introduction 1

Day 1 - Create a cozy nook 4

Day 2 - Inspire yourself and dream of better days .. 7

Day 3 - Scent the air with music 10

Day 4 - The joy of getting things done 13

Day 5 - Go on a health retreat 17

Day 6 - Keep in touch with technology 20

Day 7 - Lockdown chic 22

Day 8 - Welcome colour 24

Day 9 - Read a good book 27

Day 10 - Create something 30

Day 11 - Sort your photos 33

Day 12 - Keep the faith 37

Day 13 - Have things to look forward to 39

Day 14 - Rest when you need to................. 41

Day 15 - What will you change after this time? 43

Day 16 - Use your nice things 45

Day 17 - Set your goals 47

Day 18 - Learn something 50

Day 19 - Find your favourite comedy 53

Day 20 - Be a bright spark 55

Day 21 - Make do and mend 57

Day 22 - Self talk 59

Day 23 - Create order 61

Day 24 - Go with the flow 63

Day 25 - Move it baby! 65

Day 26 - Take a nap 68

Day 27 - Luxurious mornings 70

Day 28 - Take the wins 73

Day 29 - Be different to everyone else 75

Day 30 - Future plans 78

Bonus Day - Being feminine around the home 81

Bonus Day - Keep the home fires burning 84

21 ways to be chic at home during difficult times . 87

A note from the author 96

About the author 99

Introduction

This book was inspired by the global lockdown in early 2020, which I think I can safely say took us all by surprise. One minute we were living life and doing our thing, the next, most of us were advised to stay at home for a month or more.

If you are a reader of my blog 'How to be Chic' or follow me on social media, you might have seen my '30 Chic Days Series' on making the most of staying at home. I have spent several weeks confined to the home. We all have.

As a happy introvert, I wasn't too bothered about this, but I know it's been tough on many. Job uncertainty; home-schooling children; working from home while looking after toddlers. And then there are the brave souls working in hospitals and medical centres, in supermarkets and providing other essential services. They have received well-deserved thanks all around the world.

I am not on the front-line, but I wanted to do

something. So I commenced my fifth blog series of '30 Chic Days' and focused it on the home, self-isolation and being in quarantine... with my twist.

My writing is all about living a simple, beautiful and successful life without spending a lot of money. I enjoy decorating my home on a budget, having a 'make-do and mend' mindset, being creative, and dreaming up my own inspiration.

All of these topics I wanted to share with you, my reader. Perhaps one idea or suggestion could spark off a new course of action, or brighten up your day. I know it doesn't seem as important as, say, sewing face-masks or delivering meals to older folk who cannot leave their home, but we all serve in our own way. And this is how I have felt called to serve.

After finishing the series, I knew it needed a wider audience and hence this book was created. I have polished up the daily entries and added to them where appropriate. In addition, at the end of this book I leave you with *21 Ways to be Chic at Home* – a summary of inspiring ideas and points to have you feeling more buoyant.

I find with inspiration that it helps my state of mind enormously. Things can seem heavy and insurmountable, but then with a fresh perspective, suddenly the sun comes out and you are feeling brighter.

This doesn't just apply during a once-in-a-lifetime pandemic situation either. In all hard times, whether it is a divorce, death of a loved one or loss of a job or business, there is grief. But there is also always tomorrow. A better day. A day for living. I know this because I have lost two close family members – my father, and brother – at different times, and I have been divorced also.

I will always miss those who are no longer with us; that can't be changed. The divorce? Well, it wasn't my choice at the time, but I can now say that life has turned out to be better than I could ever have imagined in those dark days. It's brilliantly sunny for me now, and it's always a beautiful day in my world.

And so it is with our global situation. It's hard, really hard. And one of the most difficult things is not knowing when the ending is or how things are going to turn out. But we only have today, so let's make it a good one.

It is my wish that this book cheers you on, gives you new ideas to thrive with, inspires your creativity and helps you to carry on. You already have the magic within you, and I can't wait to share all of my inspiration to help you bring it out.

With all my best!

Fiona

Day 1 -
Create a cozy nook

I don't need much of a push to hibernate away, introvert-style. It just comes over me and I want to hunker down in my home, having minimal contact with the outside world. It feels a bit impolite but sometimes it's the only thing I can do. I'm learning (slowly) not to judge it, and just flow with it. (It feels like I'm playing hooky.)

During the pandemic though, the whole world has joined me in self-isolation, in their own homes of course.

Home is where many of us will be spending time for the foreseeable future. And we're the lucky ones! I know there are many who have to go to work, and I agree, it's scary times.

I don't want to give in to the fear though, and for that reason I have decided to focus on the positive things: being light-hearted, doing things around the house that I've not gotten around to, and generally making this a time of productivity and forward movement as much as possible.

Yes, I definitely spent an evening with a news program rolling live on YouTube and while it was quite fascinating to watch, it didn't feel good afterwards. I'm watching the news more because it's an unprecedented time we are in and we have to keep informed, but I'm also going to focus on the lovely.

My plan is to have little bursts of inspiration and happiness to make the most of my confinement, and to take my mind off things. It's all too easy to invite anxiety in the door when I think too much about the possibilities; I know that from personal experience and you may too.

Taking the time to tidy up loose ends and bothersome things is an excellent focus which will make you feel better (I go into more detail about this in *Day 4*). The more we are in control of things, the stronger we feel. There is so much outside of our control right now, but if we can keep order and a feeling of wellbeing near us, that's got to help.

I am often inspired by decor images where a corner has been repurposed from an empty space, into a lovely little sitting area with one or two chairs and a tiny table. Add a few flowers in a small vase, a cup of tea and a glossy picture book and you have yourself a cozy nook. I have just such a nook in my living area and it's so nice to sit there, even by myself, for a hot drink.

Another nook idea I love is to wrap up in bed (a mental nook rather than a physical one, perhaps). Each morning I have a big cup of tea delivered to me – I know, so lucky, but I'd happily get it myself if I had to – and I take this time to read something inspiring before I have my shower. I would get up earlier just to fit this time into my day if necessary.

And while you're in your cozy nook, how about **reading the books you already have**, and making the most of them? With libraries being closed around the place, it's a nice opportunity to browse your own bookshelves. I have a small number of large-format glossy picture books that I have bought or been gifted over the years, and it's not often that I take them down and read them. I asked myself, 'If not now, then when?'

While writing this chapter I inspired myself with my beloved copy of Vicki Archer's 'My French Life'. Today I read the chapter on French women and how they approach beauty and style ('Le Femmes', starting on page 61) and it was a beautiful way to start my day.

Chic Self-Care Tip: You too may already own at least one book that you could browse for a small pocket of beauty to lift your mind above the hurt. Why not go there with a cup of tea right now?

Day 2 -
Inspire yourself and dream of better days

Something fun I have been doing since I bought an iPad several months ago, is to upload my saved screenshots to my *Pinterest* inspiration boards. There are so many reasons why I love doing this:

- You get to declutter your camera roll, restoring extra space to your phone.

- Your images are saved and organized for future reference (I lost a whole lot of inspiration photos off my last laptop when it unexpectedly died, which I was very sad about).

- You get to revisit inspiration that moved you at an earlier time (and if it doesn't move you now, you can just delete it instead of uploading it).

- You can view your images from any device. I might save to Pinterest on my desktop computer or iPad, but can then view something I am trying to remember on my phone while out.

- Over time you see a beautiful pattern of what inspires you most when all your images are saved in one place.

When I feel like some relaxing time with my iPad and a cold drink, I go somewhere positive now - viewing and thinking about what inspires me - rather than to a gossipy newspaper site. It becomes a good default.

I still have quite a few screenshots on my phone, and the plan which has been working well is to declutter and save, in little chunks of time here and there. You don't need to have all your Pinterest boards available to the public either. When you save some boards as 'Private' you don't need to worry that people will judge your taste. You can save away to your heart's content and honour your true self!

The alternative to Pinterest, of course, is the old-fashioned idea which I love as well. As I read my magazines, I tear out pages which inspire me. Then, every so often, I go through the pages and put them into my style-files. I have separate files for home décor, my ideal wardrobe, positivity and success; so many places that I love to visit for inspiration.

When you read through these pages again it's like an advertisement-free magazine created especially for you. Creating your own style-file is also a great way to clean out your magazine stack too. What better way to be productive and have fun in quarantine?

Chic Self-Care Tip: Open up or start your own Pinterest account online and enjoy inspiring yourself today.

Day 3 -
Scent the air with music

I am a big fan of playing soothing, relaxing music while I am at home. It's almost as if I am scenting the air with the fragrance of music. My favourite is the kind of music you would hear in a spa or at a yoga retreat. By having this type of music on softly in the background I find it easier to be calm, stay soothed and have a peaceful state of mind for the most part.

There are different kinds of relaxing music so don't worry if you don't like whale sounds or the flutey type; you can choose classical adagios, piano music or elegant strings.

Let me introduce you to some of my favourite artists in this genre.

My number one favourite is Hilary Stagg. He plays an electric harp and I find his music calms me instantly. My number two is Kevin Kern, who plays beautiful piano music. And my third favourite is Peder Helland, who has quite ethereal music.

You can listen to their music (and others, by searching for 'relaxing music' or 'study music') on YouTube, or Spotify, my new favourite service. I have just finished my three month's free introductory offer on Spotify and now happily pay $15 per month for it. You can play pretty much anything! I decided that it was worth the monthly cost when I saw that it was less than the price of one album on iTunes.

You can also access the free version of Spotify if you want to use it without paying, but you do get advertisements sometimes.

I first came across my main favourite Hilary Stagg from a CD I was given almost twenty years ago when I worked for Parfums Christian Dior. We were sent a stack of CDs from Christian Dior in Paris to play during customer facials. It was the most beautiful music and I was entranced by it. You couldn't buy this CD anywhere and the tracks weren't listed, so I never knew who the artists were. It was an 'in-house' release.

Only recently I thought to use the Shazam app on my phone, which is fantastic for seeing what a song is that you love the sound of. I am always using it in shops and cafes and have found loads of new music this way. So I Shazam-ed all the songs on the Dior CD and have recreated it as a playlist on Spotify. If you would like to listen to my Dior CD too, you can find it by searching for 'Dior relaxing music' and you'll see it under my name 'Fiona Ferris' on Spotify. Using Shazam is how I found out that the beautiful electric harp tracks on this CD are by Hilary Stagg.

I have played this list so often now that I know the tracks off by heart, and only a few seconds into it I can feel my shoulders relax and my blood pressure drop. I hope you love the Dior playlist as much as I do!

Chic Self-Care Tip: Play your favourite music often, and let it contribute to your wellbeing.

Day 4 -
The joy of getting things done

During this time at home, I have been continuing on with my quest to simplify, declutter, organize and streamline my surroundings. To get a handle on everything that would make my life feel free and easy, I brainstormed a big list of '*Loose Ends and Bothersome Things*' (that's actually what I called it).

My financial paperwork was messy; I needed to get my tax information to the accountant for her to complete my end-of-year financial statement; my food areas – pantry, fridge and freezer – needed an inventory and clean out where I commit to making meals out of what I already have in stock; mending to be done; visits to people I hadn't seen in ages; replacing my laptop before it died; getting a new iron and microwave, unjamming my overlocker (serger) and tidying my sewing room (yes, again. Sewing rooms are never tidy for long, or at least mine isn't).

It was refreshing to create this list, because all the tasks no longer clogged up my head. Even the littlest things building up can slow you down mentally. They hang over your head like a grey cloud, even if it's a tiny weeny grey cloud such as making a phone call to book a dental check-up (which is still on my list).

After feeling stuck and not knowing where to start, I had an inkling to choose the one item that bothered me the most. Looking through my list I saw an online order where I wasn't happy with the quality. I was just going to put the items away and chalk it up to experience, but in that moment I decided to do an instant chat with the company concerned. Within a short time they had issued a credit and I didn't even need to return the items.

This win gave me the oomph to choose another thing from my list, and another. I haven't finished yet, but I have done so much already and it feels fantastic. Each mini-achievement spurs you on, I have found.

Here are the kinds of things I have been working on recently:

- I have sent tax information to my accountant for the last financial year.

- I am fully up to date with this financial year's information and will be ready to hand it over after the 31st March year-end date.

- I have filed or shredded loads of paperwork.

- I booked a plumber in to fix a number of issues that were small but irritating. None of them were big enough for a job by themselves, but when we had several, it was such a joy to see them all fixed within a day.

- Cleaning out my email Inbox and setting up 'rules' for the few mailing lists I am on. Emails from those people go into a folder which I can browse at my leisure. I've had 'getting control of my Inbox' on my wish list for years.

- My food supplies had been organized and were being used, but… then I did a stock up early this week just in case; so my pantry, fridge and freezer are all full again. However, I know this is only temporary and it has made me appreciate having space to breathe in my kitchen! (I am also grateful I can stock up, I know some don't have the funds to do that.)

- Committing to not buying certain categories until I use the last one up. Body products are a big one for me. I love pretty soaps, body lotions and fragrance. Our bathroom may or may not resemble a retail store… it's tough for me to say no to a new purchase, but it feels good to clear space over time, so I am being strong.

We are in a period of time when we will all go out less, so it's a great chance to do these kinds of things. It's incredible how good it feels to free your mind of mental clutter, and remove things from your To-Do List. Even if it's just deciding that you don't want to follow through on that item anymore and can simply cross it out.

Chic Self-Care Tip: Instead of feeling shut in, why not take pleasure from making your home orderly, and a nice place to be – let it a sanctuary for you and your family.

Day 5 -
Go on a health retreat

When my country, New Zealand, went into full lockdown for a minimum of four weeks, it happened suddenly. Just a few days' notice was given, and essential businesses such as supermarkets and chemists were the only places allowed to be open. All other stores, as well as schools, libraries and businesses closed.

Everyone was told they must stay at home, unless it was to buy groceries or be outside for exercise. There was to be no visiting people and we were asked to have as little contact with others as possible. We all understood that we must do our bit to avoid the virus getting out of control in our country.

When this time of isolation was suddenly upon us, it made me think of an experience my brother had, twelve months previous. He went on a month-long health retreat at a place called FitKoh in

Thailand. There were yoga and gym workouts and a Thai yoga massage daily. Healthy meals were provided too. It was all part of the package. He loved it, and came back fitter, healthier and refreshed.

I had already had the thought to do this for myself but without leaving the country, or even my own home. Like a Do-It-Yourself health retreat. And of course, wouldn't self-isolation be the perfect opportunity to put something like this into place? There would be no distractions from the outside world, and it could almost feel like you were in a remote part of Thailand...

I felt energized by the thought of:

- Cozying up for early nights with a good book.

- Prepping lots of nutritious food at home - making soup, chopping vegetables for salads and dinner, putting together slow-cooker meals, smoothies for breakfast, and sometimes special restaurant-style meals for dinner.

- Going on walks, and doing outdoor fitness like people do in parks, but on my own lawn.

- Yoga and stretching in my living room. I love to stretch at my own pace and just do what feels good, and I also love the *Rituals Cosmetics Global* channel on YouTube for their soothing yoga classes.

- Choosing non-alcoholic drinks more often than not.

- Doing at-home facials, and self-massage as I apply my body lotion each day.

Imagine coming out of this global self-isolation feeling healthy and vibrant, instead of having soothed your fears with chocolate and brandy and feeling not so good. I chose not to have any of my usual treat foods in the house and don't plan on stocking up at all. If I really, really want something I'll get it, but I'm not having foods available 'just in case', because, of course, when they're there, they'll get eaten. I've proven that to myself many a time.

I purposely didn't buy any brandy before the bottle stores closed down for a month either. If I want a wine I'll have one, but last night I enjoyed a flavoured sparking mineral water in a champagne flute, and it was perfect.

Chic Self-Care Tip: Are you with me? Claiming this strange and worrying time as your own personal health retreat? We can do it!

Day 6 -
Keep in touch with technology

Being at home more, I started thinking about people I wanted to keep in touch with. It wasn't a conscious decision, but something that came about organically because of our changed circumstances. Some people on my list I talk to regularly, and some I haven't spoken with in a long time.

But at times like this you want to check in with people. I've already spoken on the phone to two elderly family members who don't live near me, and I have others to contact, some by phone and some by email who are overseas. It's just nice to say 'I've been thinking about you', and it feels good to have a little catch up.

I also thought of using Facetime (or other video chat services and apps that are available) to have a coffee date or glass of wine with a friend. That would be quite fun, no? Meeting at 3pm or 5pm with a hot or cold drink, and a chat for half an hour? With video it gives you a reason to put a pretty top on and do your hair and it really feels like you are with that person. But you're still self-isolating and keeping everyone safe.

So today I'm going to add to my list of people to keep in touch with, and go through it one by one over the coming weeks. There are actually a lot of really nice side effects to this dreadful crisis, and one of them is the increased connection. I've heard of people helping others in supermarket queues (holding their place if they've forgotten something) and being kinder and more forgiving to one another in general.

May it continue long after we all get back to our normal lives!

Chic Self-Care Tip: Make your own list of people you want to say 'Hi!' to, and tick one off each day.

Day 7 -
Lockdown chic

My husband Paul said something so funny the other day. He was getting ready to go into work to get business email put on his private laptop and collect other things so he could work from home, and he looked really smart having changed into a linen shirt and dark jeans to do so. I said he looked nice, and his response? "No point in letting coronavirus get in the way of your fashion standards."

I so agree (and how awesome is Paul)! Even though we are in lockdown and aren't going anywhere, I applied simple makeup and fixed my hair like I always do, plus put on some earrings. It just feels better. Of course, perfume is a must as well.

I know this is a serious situation, but surely we can all have a little bit of Lockdown Chic in our lives while we ride out the virus?

It's fun to put together a capsule wardrobe of

home-loungewear/day-clothes-hybrid which lets you be comfortable but also feel productive and pretty. Some days I'll wear jeans and a nice top, but more often I'll be in leggings and a tee-shirt, with a long cardigan if it's nippy. All of these pieces are fairly new so they still look good, and they go in the wash often, of course.

Pairing these more casual clothes with good grooming is how I will be approaching our confinement at home. It is a different time currently, and normally I wouldn't wear leggings during the day because I come and go (and choose not to wear leggings beyond the gate.)

So to wear leggings during the day feels like a treat, but I also look pulled together when the neighbours go past walking their dogs if I happen to be outside. In a way it feels like comfort dressing, which is definitely better for you than comfort eating (I bitterly regretted having no potato chips in the house last night though, but it does mean that my plan of not stocking up on snack foods is working!)

Chic Self-Care Tip: I invite to you curate your Lockdown Chic look and rock it. Yay for comfort and style co-existing beautifully!

Day 8 -
Welcome colour

Having extra daily doses of colour was one of my ideas for this series of 30 Chic Days, and I was tickled to hear from a reader of her similar thought:

"I have been using our lockdown to flaunt much brighter makeup colors than I would normally feel comfortable leaving the house in. I feel like I'm still making the effort, that I'm using up the colors in a set that would normally go to waste, and my kids get a kick out of it!"

Isn't this a great idea? When we are confined to the home is a perfect time to try new makeup looks. I usually use a neutral eyeshadow but I'm going to do the same. I'm sure we all have those brighter colours that are in mixed eyeshadow palettes and we never get around to using them.

When I wanted to get better with eye makeup (as described in 'Day 4: Make up your eyes' in my book *Thirty Chic Days*, I practised my smoky eye makeup every day for quite a while. Some days I really rocked it too. My husband got used to coming home to a bombshell each night!

If you don't fancy the eye makeup technique, other colourful ways to brighten up your life are:

- Changing cushion covers or cloth dinner napkins out (maybe you sew and have some fabric you could use?)

- Wearing red or hot pink lipstick with simple eye makeup (matte or semi-matte feels modern and looks great in bright colours.)

- Flowers, of course. Perhaps from your garden, or faux silk flowers.

- Wearing your brighter tops and scarves to highlight your face with colour.

- Planting brightly coloured flowering plants in pots or your garden, or taking cuttings from other plants to spread colour. I love geraniums and they really are very simple to grow, even for a novice gardener like me.

- Filling your Pinterest boards with images in your favourite shades, then browsing them for an inspiring coffee break.

- Making brightly coloured salads to accompany your meals. I find that I don't often choose to have salad, but if wash and chop salad vegetables ahead of time and put a little side salad with my meal I happily eat it.

- Adding contrasting edible garnishes to meals, such as capsicum (bell pepper) slices, parsley, sliced tomatoes, carrot batons etc. They bring a crispy freshness to enhance any meal. As with salad, prepare them ahead of time and you'll be less tempted to skip them.

It doesn't have to be all about the bright colours either, although I do love to wear my tangerine coloured ballet flats and Kelly green tee-shirt with jeans. Choose whatever colours make you feel happy. I love to go all feminine and floaty sometimes. I love shades of pink at the moment and enjoy mixing up rose gold, melon, coral, pale yellow, pink and red together; all the shades of the best kind of sunrise.

I don't know if there is any scientific evidence that colour boosts your immune system but I feel like there must be, because colour feels so good.

Chic Self-Care Tip: Think about your favourite shades and how you can add more of them into your life right now.

Day 9 -
Read a good book

One of my very favourite self-soothing activities is to get engrossed in a novel. I love non-fiction, and of course the books I write are non-fiction, but there's nothing like a good story to carry you away.

A recent read was 'Grown Ups' by Marian Keyes and it was SO GOOD. I do like a satisfying read. After that I went back to Penny Vincenzi's 'A Question of Trust'. I put it down half-read for 'Grown Ups' because to be honest it wasn't the fastest moving book (but I knew it would be good so I persevered.)

Penny is well known for writing really, really long books; 'A Question of Trust' is over 600 pages. Thank goodness it was on my Kindle is all I can say; imagine holding that paperback up in bed to read it. My favourite from this author so far was 'A Perfect Heritage' which is set in the cosmetic world in 1950s London. Delicious.

And before 'Grown Ups' I read 'What Happens Now' by Sophia Money-Coutts. Oh my, she is so funny. This is her second book and I love both of them. She is obviously very posh (how can you not be with that surname?) and her books are quite posh too, but wickedly funny and quite rude in parts.

Aside from these kinds of fiction, I also love a good psychological thriller to scare me a little. The most recent book I finished was 'The Housekeeper' by Natalie Barelli and it was great to race through the book to see how it would end up.

Another excellent book in the same genre that I still remember was 'Behind Her Eyes' by Sarah Pinborough. That book still has me wondering about the possibility described within. Very creepy but I'd totally recommend it!

Isn't it fantastic that we have these make-believe worlds to disappear into when the news all gets too much? I love that feeling you get when you are so happy with the book you are reading, and you can't wait to get back to it.

I often find that I can enjoy a book more by reading it faster too. When I think a book is too slow for me (like poor old Penny's), it's because I have been *reading* it too slow. Ten minutes at bedtime is not going to get me through any book and keep up my interest!

That happened with 'Grown Ups' actually. For whatever reason I didn't give it a good start and so thought I wasn't that into it. But I put my foot on the accelerator and became wrapped up in the story, and I'm so glad I did.

As far as non-fiction goes, I enjoyed listening to the audiobook of Angela Kelly's book 'The Other Side of the Coin'. It was fascinating to hear her behind-the-scenes account of being the queen's dresser for 25 years.

Chic Self-Care Tip: At the moment when there is so much going on around us, it is even more important than normal times to find a book you enjoy, and dive into it. I am always getting ideas for new titles from book reviews in magazines, and from people I follow on Instagram. Also, the Top 100 lists on Amazon are great for finding a new read.

Day 10 -
Create something

I don't know if there is a bigger fan of 'making things' than me. Well, I'm sure there are, but I'd be right up there definitely. Mum always told us when we were growing up that 'bored people are boring people', so we'd stop bugging her when we were 'bored', and find our own entertainment. She did us well with that advice.

There are endless things you can create around your home when you have time on your hands. Even if you don't have that much extra time between working from home and home-schooling, making something takes you into a meditative space.

Even a small amount of time each day will bring benefits to your wellbeing and it's nice to intersperse television watching, with something that makes you feel like you've achieved something.

Depending on what kinds of supplies you already have at home you could:

- Start writing your book

- Knit a garment

- Sew something

- Do cross-stitch

- Bake cookies or bread

- Use craft kits you have stashed away

- Complete a jigsaw puzzle

- Take cuttings from your garden and plant them in bare spots (I have this planned for my geraniums)

- Colour in, paint or draw

I remember dad buying my sister and me balsa wood and tissue paper airplane kits when were young, maybe ten or twelve. I loved making mine. It was very satisfying to follow the instructions and create a model airplane. I don't think my brother got one because he was quite a bit younger, but my sister and I rocked our craft kits!

And can I just nag, I mean gently encourage, you a bit on the first point - to start writing your book. I know there are tons of you keen to do this (but you haven't started yet), because over the years I've had many emails about this wish.

There has never been a better time to write your book. If you need some inspiration and motivation, please join my free email class on becoming an author. There are action steps and tips over the course of three weeks - a new email every few days. Perhaps that would spur you on?

You can join that free email course by typing this in: eepurl.com/cokN39
(please note it's a 'zero', not an 'o' after the c)

As for me, I'm busy with my writing, and may well bake some gluten-free cookies. I don't have a favourite recipe as I rarely bake, so I'll just google something when I'm in the mood. I have gluten-free flour, butter, sugar and some dark chocolate to chop into slivers, so I should be right, hopefully!

Chic Self-Care Tip: Whatever you do, make it something small and achievable, or perhaps you'd rather set a big audacious goal and make a start at it. Find something that makes your heart lift with excitement and do *that*.

Day 11 -
Sort your photos

Today I sorted through a big tin of photos brought home from my dad's place after he died, and put them all into one album. I have a great method that I have used before with success.

Luckily I had two new photo albums that I bought almost six months ago for this job, yes, six months ago! If you don't have stockpiled photo albums like I do, you may be able to repurpose one you already have, or else have all your photos ready to go into an album once you can get to the shops. You can also store photos in a box, ready to flip through when the mood takes you.

Here is my not-yet-patented photo-sorting method:

Firstly **tip all your photos out on the floor**, facing up so you can see them, of course!

Then, **put face-down in a 'throw away' pile** out to the side, any photos that:

- Are blurry

- Are of people you don't know

- Give you a bad feeling

- Bring back unhappy memories

- Etc, etc.

You can be quite ruthless here, because you don't have to get rid of the 'throw away' pile just yet. You can leave it to marinate in a bag for a week or two before you throw it into the bin if you want.

After that, start **sorting photos into rough piles**. I go by decades firstly, and within that, holidays, occasions and photos you can see were taken on the same day.

Once you've done your rough piles, **start with the oldest pile and put them in the album first**. Put them into date order as well as you can without dithering too much. Do your best while working fast and just get them into the slots (I prefer cellophane slots over stick-on pages for everyday albums versus something like a wedding album where you might want it to be a bit more special and designery). You can always refine the order of photos once you've finished if you want to but I found I never did. They were fine as they were.

Remember the saying 'Done is better than perfect' to keep you going.

Then **move onto the next oldest pile and put them in the album**. As you go, try and keep like photos or occasions together. Throw out any duplicates (or put them aside for family/friends who might like them too) and take this opportunity to throw out any more photos that you wonder why they aren't in the 'throw away' pile already.

Keep on going and **before too long your floor will be clear**, except for the face-down 'throw away' pile. If you must, have a quick flick through these photos before you put them into a rubbish bag, just to make sure you haven't thrown out a keeper. You will very quickly see that none of these photos are very interesting to you.

Amazingly enough all of this doesn't take very long. My batch today took a couple of hours, but even if you have tons of photos you'll get it done within a day I'm sure, or perhaps a couple of sessions split over two days.

It's such a nice feeling to have this job done. I've gone from one big tin of photos and two crusty old albums to one nice, new album which is fun to flick through because it's in chronological order and contains only the best and nicest photos of people, pets and places. There are no more far-away blurry giraffes from a family zoo visit in the 1980s!

Chic Self-Care Tip: Have I convinced you to sort out your photos yet, or perhaps you are already filed and ready to view? Going through your photos really does make you appreciate them more too. It's great to have memories.

Day 12 - Keep the faith

The situation we are in cannot go on forever, and the same is also true for any other hard time. The sun always comes out after rain. Our job is to keep ourselves safe at the same time as keeping our faith. Be in touch with what's happening but don't wallow in the news. It feels much better to keep the spirit positive and to marinate in goodness, humour, kindness and grace.

Whenever I feel unsure of things, I look at what's going well, running my mind through all the good things in my life. Doing this never fails to lift my vibration, and with that higher consciousness comes fresh ideas and new hope.

Chic Self-Care Tip: You will not do yourself or anyone else any good by dwelling on what terrible things may happen. None of us knows. Instead, float your thoughts and intentions out into the atmosphere like pink and yellow balloons filled with happiness. Fill the world with your love. Every little bit counts.

Day 13 -
Have things to look forward to

Even though we're all in the same 'boat', not all of our situations are equal. For every one of us is in confinement at home, there is someone else who has to commute to a workplace, and that workplace could be stressful or even a health risk. What can we do if we are that person? When it seems like the end of the week is so far away, how can we cope with long-term prospects?

This is quite possibly the toughest thing any of us might have to endure in our lifetime. I can't pretend tough times I've had in the past can even compare, but it's all I have so here we go.

When the future seems bleak, it always helps me to have things to look forward to. It works best when there is a combination of big things and little things. Little things like a cold drink and half-an-hour with a magazine before dinner, or a bar of chocolate, and big things like a hobby project or... in the old days it would have been planning a holiday. But I think many of us won't be going on holiday for *quite* a while so we'll have to choose new shiny plans to keep our spirits up.

I think at this time it is more helpful to keep treats small, achievable and close. A new-to-us series on Netflix. An Instagram scroll of accounts that make us feel good. Thinking of all the things we are grateful for. I mean, the fact that we have the Internet makes a global lockdown that much more manageable. We can keep in touch with each other, and see how people in different countries are getting on. We also have entertainment at our fingertips.

For me at the moment, the things I have in my 'Look Forward To' basket are my writing projects: a new cover for my book 'Financially Chic' (done!), finishing up my new book 'The Chic Author' (almost there) and writing chapters for 'Thirty Chic Days, Vol. 3' (in progress).

I also love my reading time first thing in the morning in bed (before my shower), and before dinner on the sofa.

Chic Self-Care Tip: Take a moment to note down as many little things as possible that you could look forward to. And if you are someone who has to go to work at the moment, I salute you. Thank you for everything you are doing.

Day 14 -
Rest when you need to

I don't know about you, but I've been taking it easy more than usual. I do my chores and any jobs that need doing, but I haven't been packing tons into every day. I've been honouring my energy levels and, when they are lower, I'll rest. Whether it's sleeping an extra hour in the morning, turning in early at night, or snuggling up under a rug on the sofa and closing my eyes for a bit, the little bits and pieces of rest and repose here and there feel so good.

Strangely enough, even with all the worry in the world, I've been sleeping quite well. I think because there is such a huge event going on right now that all the little things which normally niggle me at 3am seem so insignificant!

I always know intellectually that resting is good, but I very rarely do it. Instead, I'll eat something for energy. Yes, I know, it sounds so silly when I write it down. But at the moment I am resting as a first response.

And the opposite of rest, while being the same (they both give you energy), is going for a walk. I've never seen so many people walking up and down our street. All the neighbours at one time or another. And I notice it the few times I've been out in the car as well - family groups and happy pets out walking. I think it's fantastic!

Chic Self-Care Tip: How about you? Are you able to rest more? Walk outdoors? Please take the time to rest when you need to.

Day 15 -
What will you change after this time?

I can see that many of us will take this time of forced confinement and realize that a lot of good has come from it. Yes, definitely, a lot of stress, health worries and financial strain, but also a silver lining. I know for myself there are things I will take forward and changes I will make.

I heard a lady on YouTube say that she was cooking more for her and her sixteen year-old son and that they actually sat down and had dinner together at night, because they had the time and both wanted to. She planned to do this more often in the future. I read on Twitter that someone was taking their time to shower and groom in the morning and they loved it. Me too, I have definitely been loving my morning shower time.

The main one for me right now is a renewal of my vows (he he, I just felt that was appropriate) for my love of writing - both in my books and on my blog. I don't know what it was but I felt I'd lost my spark a bit. Every so often I'd wonder if I was still 'writing in the right direction' but really, the only way you can find that out is to write about what you want to and see where it takes you. And when I am writing at the moment, guess what, it's what I've already been writing about. Yay! It is so nice to have that confirmed.

I also wonder if people who have been lucky enough to have had time off work will wonder if what they are doing is what they really want to be doing. Yes, this year is certainly one of change, I think we can all agree on that. Both forced change, and afterwards, possibly choosing our change.

Chic Self-Care Tip: What will you be taking forward? Are there any changes you think you might make afterwards? Look at the things you have both added into and deleted from your life and see if you want to make any of these changes permanent. Now is the perfect time to plan your reinvention!

Day 16 -
Use your nice things

Being in lockdown, I have been using more of my nice things. On a 'normal' day in the past, I would use my everyday things, but at the moment it feels like the time to make every day a little sparklier. Sort of like someone in jail wanting to decorate their cell a bit :)

I am wearing my Aerin 'Tuberose Le Soir' fragrance.

Sipping a glass of bubbles while I write this post (it is later in the day, just so you know!)

Trying different eye makeup looks each morning.

Wearing jewellery even though the only outing is to walk the dogs.

Lighting my new Ecoya 'French Pear' candle which was a recent gift.

Having my morning coffee from a blue and white china cup and saucer instead of the usual mug that goes in the dishwasher. It feels so fancy!

And when I finish this chapter I am going to sit down with my *Hello* magazine which arrived in the mail yesterday. How blissful.

Chic Self-Care Tip: Find all those areas in your life that you can upgrade for free by using your more special items. A nicer top, the fancy lemon-infused olive oil or the luxury body cream you got for your birthday. Doing this makes it feel like it is your birthday and you have received these lovely things as a gift. It really does make them (and you) feel brand new!

Day 17 - Set your goals

No matter your current situation, it is important to have goals to look forward to once we get back to normal. I know 'normal' will probably look quite different in the future, but it is still our lives we are getting back to and it is good to have direction.

I love the 'Now, Next, Future' goal idea, and have done this for myself many times. You can probably guess from the title that there are three sections to consider:

Now: Things you want to achieve right now. Basically things you are working on... 'now' (if you want to clarify it for when things aren't so topsy-turvy.) For me, I have decided that it's the lockdown period.

Next: The next things on your list. They aren't far

away, but you are not currently working on them. Once you have finished with your 'Now' goals, you can enjoy moving onto your 'Next' goals.

(Don't you love my 'so basic they're ridiculous' descriptions?)

Future: Your happy pipe dreams. The things that will make the sun come out, and that you think you could achieve under perfect conditions. Your 'Future' goals will give you the motivation to keep on going.

Your goals may change over time, too. Many of my goals are writing-based at the moment, whereas a month or two ago they were mostly to do with the home. For me it is exciting that I can follow where my energy is strongest and work on those goals. 'Work' isn't the best word to use actually, because when you follow the path that is the most appealing, you more effortlessly achieve your goals and it is not difficult at all.

I actually get really excited when I think about my goals. It's like the whole world is available to you; it's a heady thought!

For my 'Now' goals I have already finalized the new cover for my 'Financially Chic' book, and the next item on my Now list is my 'The Chic Author' book which I only have the final edit and read-through to do, put a cover together with the help of my graphic designer, and publish it. Apart from this

'30 Chic Days' book, those are my main focus.

When my home was the main focus before this, I had organizing and decluttering goals to inspire me, as detailed in *Day 4: The Joy of Getting Things Done* in this book.

Chic Self-Care Tip: Have you used this goal format before? It's quite fun and motivating. Find a journal or piece of paper and pour out your Now, and Next and Future goals. Inspire yourself with your fabulous thoughts, dreams and desires. The sky is the limit.

Day 18 - Learn something

I've found that spending more time at home has inspired me to increase my rate of learning. All the things I've invested in over the years are getting a good workout (or are planned for a workout). There's just something about being at home that begs you to exercise your brain and expand your knowledge into new horizons.

Resources I am talking about include:

- Doing the online courses I've bought over the years (some I've completed, some partially, some not at all.)

- Reading the eBooks on my Kindle/iPad.

- Reading the physical books on my shelves.

- Considering trying sewing patterns that I have always put off as being 'too difficult'.

Other examples I can think of are:

- Trying a recipe that is out of your comfort zone (it seems that everyone is baking various types of bread at the moment.)

- Investigating a new form of exercise online such as yoga (I have participated in a group Skype class and also do yoga workouts with YouTube videos)

- Video chats with family and friends (it's all new to me; I had a conversation with four of us and it was so fun.)

- Choosing a subject that's always interested you and researching it online (potential 'rabbit hole' here though!)

However much time you have, it's fun to have a new project to look forward to, and who knows, by the time we're all free to come and go, you might be wearing a simple skirt you made, feeling proud to have completed all the modules on a course, or written the first draft of your book.

[Later on this year} "You look nice today". "Oh thanks, this is my new Lockdown Skirt". Imagine saying that! I think it would be quite funny :)

Chic Self-Care Tip: There are tons of free classes on YouTube on any subject you could imagine, or you could study from a book if you are the self-motivated type. Find a topic or project that excites your imagination!

Day 19 -
Find your favourite comedy

Laughter is so important at a time like this. We need to find what tickles our fancy to improve our immune system, reduce pain, connect emotionally with others, improve the flow of oxygen to our heart and brain, and all sorts of amazing things. Plus, laughing is fun and just feels good.

It is a good thing to watch silly, light-hearted feel-good movies at the moment. In addition, my husband Paul and I have been enjoying the US *Shameless* series, and we are excited for the latest series of *Schitt's Creek* to arrive because it is so funny and full of heart.

I've also been indulging in Sebastian Maniscalco's YouTube channel, little snippets here and there while I tidy up the kitchen. My friend Stephanie in New Orleans put me onto him ages ago and he always makes me laugh. His clip where he talks about self-checkouts I had to watch twice this morning, it was so enjoyable :) And the 'Why would you do that?' playlist is excellent too.

Chic Self-Care Tip: Why not indulge in your favourite comedy to unwind and have a good laugh. Do it lots, because laughter really is the best medicine.

Day 20 -
Be a bright spark

I have gone from someone who very rarely watches the news, to now being in situ on the couch at 6pm for the latest updates, as well as checking online throughout the day. It is only natural to want to keep fully abreast, but I think... I've been overdoing it. I have overdosed on scary news.

My different tack, which feels much better, is to definitely still keep in touch with what's going on. After all, it's likely the biggest situation we'll ever encounter in our lifetime (hopefully there is nothing bigger at any stage.) But also to keep looking forward. Being a bright spark in my own day as well as for others.

I am not really helping the collective morale by talking over and over about all the sad and scary things going on. Instead, I thought, why not be a bright spark? A bright spark is kind and thoughtful, and finds the positive in things. They lift others and themselves up with good energy. They find a new way to bring cheer every day.

How I plan to be a bright spark is nurture myself and those close to me in ways that are both simple and free. With connection, love, and sharing in new and fun ways. Not feeling bad about the amount I'm eating. Enjoying the funny memes that are going around. Taking refuge in good books, and having a high level of appreciation for essential workers.

I get the easy job, I get to stay home. I work from home already. I don't have any children to homeschool and I don't have to check in with a boss. I know I am lucky, so the least I can do is be a bright spark in the world.

Chic Self-Care Tip: Whether you know it or not, you will likely be a bright spark for someone else. You are holding everything together and hopefully looking after yourself as well. Make it a focus, both for yourself and others.

Day 21 -
Make do and mend

Something that never fails to buoy my spirits is to do some mending. Even one item helps! Today I sewed a button back onto a shirt, but the fabric was ripped underneath, so I had to patch that, *then* sew the button on top. It had been hanging on the back of my laundry door for many, many weeks, ironed and ready to go except for this one button. I just did it now and it took me about ten minutes. *Ten minutes.* And that includes re-threading my sewing machine with white cotton. Why wait so long, Fiona?

Not only do I have a door that is clear – there is no shirt hanging on it – but I now have an extra, wearable shirt in my closet. It feels great to get things done, and I find that often it's the littlest things that make the biggest difference to your feeling of wellbeing.

We might not have any control over the world

currently (or at any time really, when you think about it), but we can control our own home. We might have to make do right now, and it's strangely satisfying, don't you think? Substituting ingredients and coming up with new favourite recipes out of necessity?

It feels good to mend too. For many items it's not an option to buy a replacement currently, but even in normal times I love to mend something if possible. It just feels good. And the bonus is that it's totally green!

I'm going to choose one more thing to mend next. I have quite the pile, you see. Some mending, some ambitious remodelling.

Chic Self-Care Tip: Make it your mission to tidy up all those little areas of bother, like my shirt on the door, and see how good you feel.

Day 22 - *Self talk*

Today's topic is more of a... rant. Will you allow me a minute?

Okay, so here it is. I can't count the number of times I've heard the phrase 'stuck at home'. News broadcasters are particularly fond of it.

"Here's some tips for you to avoid being bored while stuck at home."

"How much longer are we going to be stuck at home for?"

"Here's how the nation has handled being stuck at home today."

And even in normal conversation with people you speak with, there's talk of 'going stir-crazy', 'having cabin fever', being, yes, 'stuck at home' and many other variations.

Firstly, if we're 'stuck at home', we're one of the fortunate ones. I'm sure frontline staff and essential workers would love to be 'stuck at home', rather than risking illness to work at a supermarket checkout or nursing sick people.

I do agree though that we are all having different experiences. If you and your family live in an apartment with not even a balcony, it would be different to me, living in the country with a quiet street to walk along in the sunshine.

And if you are an extrovert who loves to get out and about, versus being an introvert like I am who counts home as her absolute favourite place to be? I get that, it would be hard.

It's really such a great learning experience, isn't it? Working out how to best live in this new world we find ourselves in? Something I've noticed is that there is a ton of creativity being generated. Normal people creating funny music videos, inventive ways to come up with a different meal every night and even for myself, I've felt more creative and motivated.

What's up with that? Maybe when we feel squeezed in one way, it comes out in another.

Chic Self-Care Tip: Join me and change your mindset from being 'stuck at home' to, 'What a privileged life we lead'. I feel incredibly grateful to be where I am, and a bit guilty too, because I'm not on the front line. I think it's only natural.

Day 23 - Create order

Being at home almost 100% of the time at the moment, and with my husband too, means the house is used more and requires frequent picking up. This is without children; I can't even imagine how much more there would be to tidy each day with children in the house!

Our two cats and two dogs play with their toys (which can go from being neatly stashed in the toy basket to strewn everywhere in a very short time), but I know they can't compare to how 'busy' children are.

I'm not about to spend hours a day making our home picture-perfect, but a few things I do every day make all the difference (and I try to get them done as quick as possible, so I can get on with other things.)

Number one is **making the bed**. Each morning I enjoy creating order in the bedroom and doing a nice job of making our bed. It sets the scene for this room, and my day.

Number two is **the kitchen**. It makes a huge difference to have all dirty dishes in the dishwasher, and stray items put away. Sometimes I forget, and there are things left on the counter for a few days, but when I sort myself out and put everything back where it belongs, the visual calm soothes me.

Number three is **the living area** where we spend our evenings. Tidying and wiping down the coffee table, setting out a new candle for the night and putting my reading material there is nice to come into when we are ready to relax before dinner.

The good news is that the laundry isn't getting as much use at the moment with no business shirts or going-out clothes needed. Silver lining!

Chic Self-Care Tip: Think about the top three things that would make the biggest difference to your serenity and do them daily. Your calmed mind will thank you.

Day 24 - Go with the flow

Because none of us have experienced a global pandemic before (I say it so casually, but we are living history in a massive way at the moment!), we have to cut ourselves a bit of slack. There is no guidebook for this so we're all just working it out the best we can, and from my experience every day is different.

At the beginning of lockdown, I was determined to be the best me ever once we were past the worst of things. Decluttered, exercising daily without a prod, and of course, eating healthful home-cooked meals since there weren't any other options.

Some days are like that, and some... are not. Some are woefully lazy. But I've decided that 'it is what it is'. If I want the chocolate, I'll have it. And I definitely have been indulging. But also, I've been craving my veges and wanting freshness in my food. Like the body is seeking balance. Potato chips and broccoli: perfect.

I've been doing my YouTube yoga classes with pleasure too. Plus continuing with my mending pile and pottering around doing things in the home. I've found that when you take the pressure off yourself to be that perfect person, you find out what you actually enjoy doing. It's fascinating.

Chic Self-Care Tip: I hope you're cutting yourself a bit of slack today, too. Do what you do, and do it with pleasure.

Day 25 - Move it baby!

I haven't been perfect about it, but the days when I move myself with a bit more effort than just going from the bed to the shower to the couch, I feel so good. My husband Paul and I have gotten ourselves into a nice, not-too-taxing quarantine morning routine, which is: breakfast - some work - a dog walk - 'exercise class' - lunch.

So far for our exercise classes we've done yoga and Pilates classes from my favourite Rituals Cosmetics Global YouTube channel, and today we did a lower body calisthenics workout (from Megan Margot's 'At home fully body workout routine' on her YouTube channel.) I can really feel it in my thighs and dread to even consider how they will be tomorrow. I will probably be unable to walk. Onwards and upwards though!

Paul normally goes to the gym (which is closed

during lockdown) and I... don't. He's been such a good sport about doing my workouts with me and it's definitely more enjoyable than doing them on your own. If I had children I'd totally make them do workouts with me too.

The only equipment I use is a yoga mat, and Paul uses a towel because I only have one mat, so you could definitely lay a towel down on the floor. Plus we used food in cans from the pantry when I realized the Pilates video I'd chosen needed hand-weights one time. I usually search for workout videos on YouTube that say 'no equipment'. There is so much you can do without any equipment, and that's basically what 'calisthenics' is - using your own body weight to work out.

I love that doing these videos is free; you can change up who you follow or what kind of workouts you choose; do them at a convenient time, and once you get yourself in front of your television, iPad or phone, that's all you need to do. From there on someone will lead you through the workout and be your coach and motivator.

Chic Self-Care Tip: Search on YouTube for 'how I lost weight' or 'fitness journey' stories and watch a few if you need a push to start. Some will resonate and some won't, but the ones that do will spark something in you and you will be so keen to do a workout. And if I can get enthused about working out, I truly believe anyone can. I'm the least sporty person I know!

The cool thing too, is that you feel mentally well after a workout, so it's not just physical. I think we can all agree that feeling mentally better at this time is even more important than usual. We want to come out of this with our sanity intact!

Day 26 - Take a nap

One thing I've found while we have been confined to home, is that I've been really tired. Not just when I am doing a bit more exercise either (but definitely that's a small part of it.) I start nodding off about 9pm and can't wait to get into bed, and this afternoon after a cup of tea I closed my eyes for fifteen minutes sitting on the sofa. I've turned into a ninety-year-old. No offense to ninety-year olds, of course!

I've seen a great meme which says something like, 'We're in a pandemic, not a productivity contest', which I think is so good. On the one hand it's totally true, and on the other, if you're lucky enough to be at home waiting it out, there's a feeling of guilt so you want to be that productive person as well.

But the tiredness is there. Maybe it's all the thinking about things. It drains your battery. And we are coming into Autumn in New Zealand. The long shadows when it's still quite early and that sleepy weather's-getting-cooler cicada sound make me feel like rugging in for the upcoming winter. Hibernation time!

I always resist naps but they are meant to be an excellent thing to do. I don't know if I will become a napper properly, but I will certainly have one when needed, and relish my early nights too.

I was also quite interested to see in the news that many people have reported feeling very tired, so it's not just me. Apparently our global situation is part of the cause. It's the hypervigilance as much as anything. Even when we're not thinking about it, it's on our mind.

Chic Self-Care Tip: Please don't feel guilty for needing a nap, how you are feeling is completely normal apparently. Our minds are processing a lot, so it's only natural that our body will be feeling the drain.

Day 27 -
Luxurious mornings

What sets me up for a great day at home is my morning shower routine. This routine is something that has evolved – I keep adding more elements! – and I love it so much. I've always enjoyed long, hot showers, right from when I was young. It's just a nice place to be. These days I alternate a quicker shower one day with a longer one the next (the longer shower is when I wash my hair every second day.)

I make a big production of my morning shower and it's fantastic. I get up early (6am mostly), because I read in bed with tea, and then about 7am I have my shower. I enjoy using fragranced body products and like to set out what I'm going to use that day before I turn the shower on. It's sort of like laying out your clothes for the day.

There is quite the selection... I always put body butter or something thicker and richer on my feet; a normal body lotion on my legs; and a pretty scented body lotion on my arms, shoulders, stomach, and décolletage.

In the shower I have a scented soap; I love soap so much more than shower gel. I don't like to waste anything so I always stick the tiny old piece of soap to the new one. This thrills the thrifty part of me. I have a foaming cleanser for my face, and an exfoliating scrub, and I use one or the other. There is a back brush and a pair of exfoliating gloves, and I'll use at least one of these things most days.

The other favourite thing I have in my shower is a $10 Bluetooth speaker. I recharge it once or twice a week and stick it back up on the shower wall. I listen to YouTube videos and audiobooks and it makes my shower time so enjoyable.

And finally, I have a squeegee hanging on a hook in the shower, and I like to clean down the walls and doors of the shower so that the moisture is gone and it looks like new again.

When I don't have as much time, I'm in and out of the bathroom (fairly) quickly, but on a day when I do have space in my schedule it's such a pleasure. I come out of the bathroom feeling like I have visited a high-priced spa, and I am fully pumped up and motivated for the day because I have been listening to someone inspiring on YouTube!

Chic Self-Care Tip: Enhance your shower time in the morning if you have the time. Even if you can only spare ten minutes, make it lovely, and set yourself up for a brilliant day.

Day 28 - Take the wins

So, I might not have been winning at everything at the moment (chocolate and potato chip consumption going up, as well as general productivity being down.) Maybe you're the same? But by counting the good things it helps you feel good about yourself and you can get back into a momentum upswing again.

For me, I can count that:

- I have been much more creative, and (mostly) easily writing this book, getting more ideas for books, and working towards my writing goals.

- I have dressed nicely (clean and casual), and done my hair and makeup each day.

- The bed is made each morning and the laundry is up-to-date.

- Even though snack foods have been around, we have two or three healthy meals a day.

- I have been reading a lot.

- My husband Paul and I have become closer (talking about our future lifestyle, going for dog walks, and exercising together), and it's been fabulous to spend the time with him before he goes back to work.

I think we can consider ourselves winning at life, if we remind ourselves of the things we are doing well, don't you? Even when the moment is darkest, there are still bright spots we can find if we look.

Chic Self-Care Tip: I hope you note what you are doing well currently (and make peace with any spectacular failures, he he). I ate too many Scorched Almonds today and had eater's regret. Such is life :)

Day 29 -
Be different to everyone else

I've always loved being different to others, starting right back in high school when I didn't want to wear what the trendy girls were wearing. I made my own clothes and chose to be inspired by London street style rather than what the local stores were selling.

This desire continues to the present day, just in different areas of my life, and today's chapter is to encourage you to be different to others during this difficult time.

Instead of complaining about the inconvenience, being bored, wanting to meet up with people and spending time being worried and scared,

Why not:

- Be thankful for your health and your circumstances?

- Make the most of the time and learn something new?

- Be positive and a breath of fresh air when you speak to people?

- Take this opportunity to do things differently than you normally do?

- Think long-term (your five-year plan) rather than short-term ('when will we get out of lockdown?' or 'when will this difficult situation pass?')

Be unexpected, talk about things other than the virus or the difficult circumstances you are facing; ask people questions about their dreams; and read inspiring books. Of course, there will be talk of the news of the day, but don't dwell on it. Dwell in beauty and possibility instead, to paraphrase Emily Dickinson.

One of my favourite concepts is that you can live in the real world, but you don't have to be 'of' the real world. You can live here in the current moment, and create magic in your mind. Mix both together. The practical plus your own inspiration.

Chic Self-Care Tip: If you were to do something differently right now, what would it be? And, is there something small you can do to anchor the feeling of that change today?

An example of mine is that I often daydream about my ideal Parisian lifestyle (while still living my simple country life in New Zealand). I am inspired to be more chic by playing French café music, wearing red or hot-pink lipstick at home, and dressing better – how I imagine my idealistic French girl might. I channel my inner Audrey Tautou and my day is brighter.

Day 30 -
Future plans

Exciting future plans can make everything seem more bearable in the moment today. Certainly, a trip to Paris might not be on the cards for a while, but I love to have lots of little things to look forward to right here at home. In my inspiration notebook I write ideas down as I think of them; different things I've dreamed up such as:

- Making my own clothes like I used to in my teens and twenties.

- Perusing fabrics to be inspired by once the shops are open again.

- Looking through the handful of *Burda* European sewing magazines I have.

- Rewatching Nancy Meyers movies to soak in the

wonderful homes she creates.

- Making my own home more 'spa-like' in its atmosphere.

- Creating a 'capsule collection' of foods and recipes that support my healthy lifestyle.

Having fun things to look forward to really is the spice of life. They draw you forward with their promise of a better life and give you hope. My inspiration notebook is an alluring depository of all my ideas. Most days I like to start of fresh list of 'Exciting Ideas' or 'Happy Thoughts' where I list all the things that are making me feel happy or excited at that time.

There are plans such as deciding to make myself some new cushion covers from scrap fabric, keywords to inspire such as 'spa life, gentle, cocooning' and perhaps movies I've enjoyed in the past and want to re-watch for the feeling of them. Sometimes it's the movie itself, and others it is the period in time when I first watched that movie. It brings it back to me. Revisiting nostalgia feels so comforting and like a warm hug, don't you find?

For me it's all about the feeling of something. When I write about my future plans, I have good feelings that inspire my words and actions. One day that feeling might be sparky, energetic, cheeky and go-get-'em, and others it might be dreamy, soothed and calming.

Chic Self-Care Tip: Life really is a wonderful feast – there is so much goodness for us to choose from and it all starts in our mind! We can do our best with the current day *and* dream of a better future. By bringing details of that better future into our present day, we are already halfway there.

*Bonus Day -
Being feminine around the home*

Something that always helps to lift my spirits is to be more feminine around the home. I find that I feel lighter and happier. A nice side effect is that my husband Paul notices and comments on things I've done too, so that's nice.

I'm happy to share some of my favourite ways to be feminine around the home with you:

- Brushing my hair and tying a pretty ribbon around my ponytail. I found a black satin ribbon in my sewing supplies which was perfect.

- Lighting a candle, even during the day.

- Putting hand cream on, with bonus points if it has a beautiful fragrance.

- Having French music playing softly in the background all day.

- Wearing earrings - I have a favourite pair of cultured pearl stud earrings that I wear most often - my nana gave them to me for my 14th birthday, so they are 35 years old!

- Tying a silk scarf around my neck if it's chilly.

- Painting my nails - I complete the process like the nail lady I sometimes go to - a base coat, two coats of colour and a topcoat. I then set my alarm for 30 minutes and type or edit my book, being careful not to bump my nails.

- Putting on sheer, pretty makeup and fragrance.

- Cooking a delicious meal from an idea on Pinterest or a recipe I've saved.

- Spending time reading a book or crafting.

- Picking a few flowers to put in a bud vase.

I love the subject of femininity so much, that I've written chapters in my books with further ideas:

Day 13: Indulge in your femininity in 'Thirty Chic Days'
And,

Day 11: Honour your feminine heart in 'Thirty More Chic Days'

All these little things that can make us feel more feminine are free, or almost free. And they bring so much reward.

Chic Self-Care Tip: Even if you don't do everything on this list, just choose the one that looks most appealing. Or perhaps this bonus chapter has sparked other ideas for you to feel more feminine while at home.

Bonus Day -
Keep the home fires burning

Something that strikes me as very important is that we keep our home fires burning. To me this means keeping our personal lives in balance as much as possible, and focusing on our own wellbeing at the same time as looking out for others.

Not only will it stand us in good stead as time goes on and we emerge out the other side of a difficult situation, but keeping our mind centred on creating calm and order reduces stress and anxiety.

When I feel out of kilter and like things are getting on top of me, resulting in general grumpiness, it's because I feel like I have lost control of my surroundings. Not in a big way, mind you, but in all the little ways that we can forget to do things around the home.

I won't have been picking up as much, or forgotten to put out pretty touches such as a posy from the garden in a vase. I might have let my cleaning and tidying 'little and often' routine slip (my husband Paul always says that 'little and often' is the key to life.) Maybe I haven't prepped food ahead of time, and haven't kept up with the laundry so it's been piling up.

None of these things are big in themselves, but when you ignore them for whatever reason, it can feel like the world is heavy on your shoulders. I know I'm being dramatic here, but when you feel bogged down it helps no-one.

For me, a sure-fire way to feel like I'm the one in charge of my life is to start creating order, slowly and methodically. One load of washing off the line, folded and put away. Making our bed. Dishes in the dishwasher, swooshing away getting cleaned. Flower gardens watered in dry weather. Dinner decided on and ingredients to hand; maybe it's even all put together and the only thing I have to do is turn on the oven later.

There are the many domestic ways in which I keep our home fires burning. I love being at home and I love tending my home. Doing this always puts me in such a good mood, so I'm definitely a nicer person when my house is in order.

After writing this chapter I looked up the phrase, and 'Keep the Home Fires Burning' is a British patriotic song written in 1914, for soldiers in the first world war. The lyrics talk about men being away fighting and dreaming of home. The people left at home were doing their bit by having a cared for home for the soldiers to come back to.

An online dictionary said this phrase means 'To maintain daily routine and provide the necessities of life in a home or community.' I think this is such a lovely thought to keep morale high at this or any other time.

Chic Self-Care Tip: I always think that if we support our home, our home will support us. Keep your home fires burning and you will have done your bit.

21 ways to be chic at home during difficult times

I do hope you have enjoyed this petite book. To finish, I want to leave you with a 'chic summary' of sorts – my top 21 ways to feel chic at home during difficult times. Please enjoy!

1. **Keep to your routine as much as possible**. It might not be your normal everyday routine, but find one that is gentle and cosseting as well as providing boundaries to help you feel safe. Pare down your to-do list and find a balance of rest and productivity that feels right for you.

2. **Dress for the day when you rise**. Take a shower or bath, moisturize, put on perfume and makeup, do your hair and dress in something clean, comfortable and pretty. Each of these things can be done very simply, and when you

do them you will feel so much better.

3. **Prepare food ahead of time**. I love to wash and chop vegetables which are then stored in separate containers in the fridge. They can be used to make a salad, or in an omelette or stir-fry. I also make double batches of food that successfully reheats such as Spaghetti Bolognese, pasta bakes and casseroles. Add a salad or veges and you have dinner without fuss. When you prepare food ahead of time it's easier to eat healthy *and* you feel looked after.

4. **Do things that make you feel good**. For me it's getting stuck into an engrossing novel. For my husband it's watching a series on Netflix. I also find that a little craft project or doing some mending raises my mood and gives me a feeling of satisfaction.

5. **Keep your surroundings orderly**. Doing a little bit of tidying each day means your home stays neat, and a neat home promotes a grounded feeling in my book. I can happily ignore 'hot spots', where items lie around messily, for days, but when I take five minutes to identify where everything needs to go and put them there, it feels amazing! I have had a torch with dead batteries on my writing desk for days, and just before writing this chapter I put new batteries in it and put the torch away in my

husband's bedside drawer, where we will know to look for it when we need it. My desk now looks a million times better without a torch and batteries strewn around everywhere!

6. **Get some fresh air outside**. I take my dogs for a walk each day. Sometimes it's a long walk and sometimes it's a short walk. But even before we adopted our dogs, I used to love going for a walk around the neighbourhood listening to an audiobook with my headphones on. You get air in your lungs and some Vitamin D on your skin. It feels good to move your body too, and with something to listen to, you forget you're even exercising.

7. **Take the time to complete small projects**. When you have unexpected time at home, make a list of all the big and little things you've always wanted to do but never gotten around to. Those kinds of things for me are weeding the garden, tidying my bathroom cupboards, cleaning all my makeup cases and throwing out old makeup, going through my scarf collection, sorting my closet and making up a capsule wardrobe for the season. Then, when I'm feeling uninspired, I will choose one of these things and potter away leisurely. I soon get into it and before too long I have finished one task. It feels good *and* I have an area made more beautiful.

8. **Sort out your finances**. Get any tax information to your accountant, make sure your bank account reconciliations are up to date and do your will. Yes, these are all things I did during my confinement period at home. I feel great having them sorted out!

9. **Add luxe touches to your home**. I have been using my 'good' candles more, picking flowers from the garden for small vases (usually I can't be bothered, I'm sorry to say), setting the table nicely even just for the two of us and generally making things more special. It feels more like a social occasion than just 'staying at home'. I even saw one lady's idea on Instagram which I am totally stealing borrowing, and that was to have a live jazz singer playing on their television while they enjoyed an anniversary *dinner à deux* at home. It's almost as good as going out for dinner in a jazz club, which is something I have always wanted to do. Until that time, we will have Diana Krall croon to us at home.

10. **Upgrade your mindset**. Instead of bemoaning being stuck at home, change your way of thinking to one of adventure. How can you make this a fun experience? How can you take this unexpected pause and make it something amazing that you will remember fondly for years to come? When I think that way, it makes me want to write more. I imagine how

incredible it would be to create a new book for my readers and have completed it within a few months. What is that project, dream, wish or desire for you?

11. **Write a book**. While we're on the subject… have you ever wondered if you could write a book? Is it on your wish list? Why not start when you have more time on your hands (if you're that lucky). You don't need to learn, plan or research anything. Just start writing, suspend all judgemental thoughts and see what you can create. No-one needs to see it if you truly don't want them to, but what if you wrote your first book and it was the start of a new career for you?

12. **Reinvent yourself**. Whatever this difficult time is for you, whether it's the lockdown, death of a loved one or a difficult parting and subsequent new way of living, why not reinvent yourself. You can be anyone and anything you want; at any time, but particularly now. Think about who you've always wanted to be. Make inspiring notes about that person and start doing little things that she would do. You can reinvent yourself within the container of a happy life too. It's one of my favourite ways to inspire myself!

13. **Drink more water**. This is one of the easiest ways to feel physically well, but can often be

forgotten, even by me who is a champion water-drinker. I make sure I keep refillable water bottles (sometimes two!) on my writing desk. I take them with me in my car. They are by my bed at night. I always have a water glass by the kitchen sink and drink a glass when passing. I don't feel as good when even a little bit dehydrated. Water is good for everything, so keep sipping. You can also try sparkling mineral water, herbal teas and water with fruit sliced in it for a touch of luxury.

14. **Keep in touch**. Ring someone for a chat. Write them an email. Say 'I was just thinking of you and wanted to say hi'. It's so nice when someone gets in touch 'just because' and not because they want to borrow something or for you to do them a favour. Be that person for someone else. It lifts the spirits of both of you. I always feel cheered up when I get off the phone with someone I haven't talked to in a while.

15. **Have little goals to spur yourself on**. I love to set goals for myself, and the magic number seems to be three. It's a number that seems achievable. It might be three goals in a day, which for me would be to do a half-hour workout in the living room, prep dinner at lunchtime when I am making my lunch (otherwise it seems an almost insurmountable task if I leave it until 6pm) and write one

chapter. You could have three bigger goals for the week or month. I have three main projects I want to complete this month so they are my goals. One of them is this book you are reading right now.

16. **Stretch your body**. There is nothing I like better than to have a stretching session. It can be done when I'm feeling tired and lazy, and I feel immeasurably better even after five or ten minutes. I lie on my back and stretch my arms and legs long, bend one knee and do a spinal twist and generally stretch in any direction that feels good. I think I even prefer stretching to taking a nap. I feel energized and refreshed afterwards.

17. **Honour the feminine side of you**. Choose soft colours to wear, tie on a silk or cotton scarf, brush your hair and wear it out (I am guilty of wearing my hair in a ponytail too often), and at the very minimum wear earrings even if you don't wear jewellery at home. I also like to remember to walk and speak softly, and have delicate sweeping hand movements. It's almost more for me than my husband, because it feels lovely.

18. **Revisit your inspiration**. Do you have style files like I do? I have many torn-out magazine pages, some dating back decades. I have regular

clean-outs and only keep what still inspires me. It's so fun to browse style files, and almost like it is a magazine tailor-made for you. I love to come across a fresh idea and immediately put it into practice. Pinterest is the modern way and I do enjoy my Pinterest boards, but there is something about the paper pages, don't you think?

19. **Paint your nails**. Something I've been doing more of for a while now, is painting my nails and I love the effect. Whenever I see a lady with painted nails, it gives off the aura of a luxurious, pampered life, when all it takes is half-an-hour of your time. My favourite look is to cut my nails quite short – level with the ends of my fingers, push the cuticles back and paint in a bright or dark shade (always a crème shade, no shimmer). I love clear, classic red, deep plum and orange-red too. I generally do them once a week, and sometimes leave my nails free of colour for a few days in between just to let my nails breathe.

20. **Go armchair travelling**. I love to watch a movie set in Paris, London or New York City, or browse a large-format glossy travel book (I love borrowing them from the library) about another country. It feels like you have *been somewhere*. Going through past vacation photos with my husband, glass of wine in hand is fun too. You

can really get the feeling of being there and it's fun to dream of your next holiday one day in the future.

21. **Slow down your pace of life**. Something I have found is that when life is difficult or something big happens, time seems to slow down. It's as if you are being forced to focus on what matters. Once things are back to normal, it's all too easy to go straight back to how things were, but what if you took the chance to make a few intentional changes? I have had this as a focus for a while now, and even though it feels like you are going against the common grain, it feels right and natural too. Be willing to go against the norm and do what is right for you, whatever that may be.

A note from the author

Thank you for reading this book, and I sincerely hope you have enjoyed it. I wanted to create a quick-to-read guide, as well as inspiration to live serenely during the global pandemic, and I also thought that it could be helpful in other tough times in life too.

None of us knows what the future may hold, so all we can do is keep our spirits high and do our best – for ourselves, our loved ones and those around us. We could all use a heightened sense of loveliness at this time, and I trust this book has helped you to create beauty in your surroundings, with your mind, and in the way you interact with others.

I send my very best wishes to you, and if you would like to read more, I write regularly on my blog 'How to be Chic' at howtobechic.com. There, I keep you company and share my inspiration on living a simple, beautiful and successful life, no matter your circumstances or budget. This has been my goal from the start of my blog ten years ago, and it is still my focus today.

If you would like further inspiration still, I have published several books on Amazon which you can find at amazon.com/author/fionaferris. Some of my books have also been translated into Lithuanian, Russian, Vietnamese and Spanish.

I love everything about the process of writing my books. I get excited by the initial ideas I come up with, work through each chapter bringing those ideas to life, revisit the whole book in the editing phase and then create a beautiful cover with the help of my graphic designer. I love seeing a new book join the family; it's always such a thrill.

Writing about living a simple, beautiful and successful life without spending a lot of money is my happy place, and I appreciate you sharing it with me by reading this book.

If you enjoyed it, I would so appreciate an honest review on Amazon. It doesn't need to be long; just a few words would mean the world to me. Reviews, both good and bad, are so important to authors; it's how other people find their books. So if you are happy to spend a few minutes writing a review, thank you!

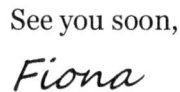

See you soon,

Fiona

About the author

Fiona Ferris is passionate about, and has studied the topic of living well for more than twenty years, in particular that a simple and beautiful life can be achieved without spending a lot of money.

Fiona finds inspiration from all over the place including Paris and France, the countryside, big cities, fancy hotels, music, beautiful scents, magazines, books, all those fabulous blogs out there, people, pets, nature, other countries and cultures; really, everywhere she looks.

Fiona lives in the beautiful and sunny wine region of Hawke's Bay, New Zealand, with her husband, Paul, their rescue cats Jessica and Nina and rescue dogs Daphne and Chloe.

To learn more about Fiona, you can connect with her at:

howtobechic.com
fionaferris.com
facebook.com/fionaferrisauthor
twitter.com/fiona_ferris
instagram.com/fionaferrisnz
youtube.com/fionaferris

Book Bonuses

http://bit.ly/ThirtyChicDaysBookBonuses

Type in the link above to receive your free special bonuses.

'21 ways to be chic' is a fun list of chic living reminders, with an MP3 recording to accompany it so you can listen on the go as well.

Excerpts from all of Fiona's books in PDF format.

You will also **receive a subscription** to Fiona's blog '*How to be Chic*', for regular inspiration on living a simple, beautiful and successful life.

Printed in Great Britain
by Amazon